# Luke
# BRYAN

*John Bankston*

Mitchell Lane
PUBLISHERS
P.O. Box 196
Hockessin, Delaware 19707
Visit us on the web: www.mitchelllane.com

**Mitchell Lane**
PUBLISHERS

Printing    1        2        3        4        5        6        7        8        9

## Blue Banner Biographies

**Library of Congress Cataloging-in-Publication Data**
Bankston, John, 1974–
  Luke Bryan / by John Bankston.
    pages cm. — (Blue banner biographies)
  Includes bibliographical references and index.
  ISBN 978-1-68020-081-2
1.  Bryan, Luke — Juvenile literature. 2.  Country musicians — United States — Biography — Juvenile literature.  I. Title.
  ML3930.B875B36 2016
  782.421642092 — dc23
  [B]
                                                                            2015017150
eBook ISBN: 978-1-68020-082-9

**ABOUT THE AUTHOR:** Born in Boston, Massachusetts, John Bankston began writing articles while still a teenager. Since then over two hundred of his articles have been published in magazines and newspapers across the country, including travel articles in *The Tallahassee Democrat*, *The Orlando Sentinel* and *The Tallahassean*. He is the author of over sixty biographies for young adults, including works on Alicia Keys, Missy Elliot, Eminem, scientist Stephen Hawking, author F. Scott Fitzgerald and actor Jodi Foster. Bankston likes different kinds of music, including country music.

**PUBLISHER'S NOTE:** The following story has been thoroughly researched and to the best of our knowledge represents a true story. While every possible effort has been made to ensure accuracy, the publisher will not assume liability for damages caused by inaccuracies in the data and makes no warranty on the accuracy of the information contained herein. This story has not been authorized or endorsed by Luke Bryan.

SONY
make.believe

Today Luke Bryan is able to enjoy all the advantages of celebrity — like attending the movie premiere of Country Strong in 2010. As a young adult, however, he sometimes wondered if he'd ever leave Georgia.

# *Country Dreams*

*L*uke Bryan wanted to play country music for a living. "I was a horrible daydreamer," he admitted on the radio program *Big D & Bubba*. For Luke, playing country music was the only dream that really mattered and by 1996 he was ready to make his dream come true.

He had already played at bars and nightclubs near his Georgia hometown. Even before he was old enough to drive, he had been paid for performing. But he wanted to turn a part-time, weekend job into a career. Luke Bryan wanted to enter a profession where many try but few succeed. For country music hopefuls there is one destination: Nashville, Tennessee.

With a population of just over 600,000 Nashville is the second largest music production center in the U.S., after New York City which has over ten times as many people. In Nashville, country music is the music of choice.

Country music features acoustic instruments (guitar, violin/fiddle, banjo) and drums, and storytelling delivered in the accents of the south. The first country recording of Texan fiddler Eck Robertson dates to 1922 and country music has been popular ever since. Three major record labels in Nashville compete to sign the most talented singers and songwriters, and Luke hoped to be one of them.

Like many country singers, Luke wanted to play the songs he wrote. When he wasn't attending school, performing, or working on his father's peanut farm, he was writing new songs.

"Some of my parents' friends drove to Valdosta to tell me and drive me back. I do believe that when my brother was born, God allocated him twenty-six years. It was his time," said Luke.

When Luke was ready to leave home to pursue his dream, his older brother Chris had a message for him. "He told me someone had called the house about me and my band playing a show," Luke told *Parade* Magazine. After hanging up, Luke drove from Leesburg to Valdosta, Georgia to see a girlfriend.

While Luke was away, Chris was killed in a car accident. Luke told *Parade* Magazine, "Some of my parents' friends drove to Valdosta to tell me and drive me back. I do believe that when my brother was born, God allocated him twenty-six years. It was his time."

Chris had encouraged Luke to pursue his music. Now that Chris was gone, so were Luke's Nashville dreams. Even as he did all he could to make his parent's lives easier, Luke wondered if his entire future had been rewritten. Instead of being a country music star, it looked like he would live out his life working in Leesburg, Georgia.

*Sometimes Luke Bryan is a headliner, sometimes he is a supporting act. Either way, he built his fan base by touring regularly — as he does here in Ontario, Canada, during his headlining "Kick The Dust Up Tour" on May 1, 2015.*

When Luke Bryan joined Florida Georgia Line members Brian Kelley and Tyler Hubbard onstage at the 2014 Billboard Music Awards it was a special night. Luke won two awards – for "Top Country Album" and "Top Country Artist."

# CHAPTER 2

# *Florida Georgia Line*

Leesburg, Georgia is more than a two-and-a-half hour drive and a world away from the city of Atlanta. A small town of just 3,000 people, Leesburg lies in the southwest portion of the state and is surrounded by dirt roads and farms. That is where country star Thomas Luther "Luke" Bryan was born on June 16, 1976. His father Tommy owned a peanut farm and worked as a fertilizer salesman. His mother LeClaire worked at the local utility company and tried hard to make a nice home for Luke and his older siblings, brother Chris and sister Kelly.

As the baby of the family, Luke was often the center of attention and singing came naturally to him. "He was sickly when he was a little baby,' his mother recalled on the ABC News program *20/20*. "I bounced him all the time and hummed 'Rock of Ages.'" Luke hummed the song before he could talk.

Growing up, Luke played baseball and loved fishing. He enjoyed his small town childhood, and for him, it was extraordinary for being so ordinary.

By the time he was a teenager, Luke was helping out on his father's farm. It was difficult work, shelling and separating peanuts at the Bryan plant. Years later, he was grateful. "When you grow up with a hard working background it prepares you for life in general," he told *The Palm Beach Post*.

> *"When you grow up with a hard working background it prepares you for life in general," said Luke.*

Music was important at home and he heard country classics by legends like Kenny Rogers, Conway Twitty, Ronnie Milsap, and music by newer stars like Clint Black. He listened to the music his older siblings enjoyed, performed by early 1980s pop and rock stars.

On his fourteenth birthday Luke received the gift that would change his life—a guitar.

By picking out the chords, he slowly taught himself how to play. It usually takes years after someone picks up a musical instrument before they are good enough to perform for money, but Luke was paid to play music before he turned sixteen. By seventeen he was a regular performer at Skinner's, a local bar that devoted one section to high school students. In the beginning, Luke mainly played covers (songs made famous by other singers). As his confidence grew, he began playing the songs he had written.

His performances weren't limited to local bars and nightclubs. He sang in the choir while attending the First Baptist Church. He also acted on stage at Lee High School in plays like *Annie Get Your Gun*. "He could just fill up a room," Robby Davis, the school's theater director told *Parade* Magazine.

After graduating from high school, Luke attended Darton State College in Albany, Georgia. For Luke, pursuing a country music career was more important than classes. He already had an apartment lined up in Nashville before Chris was killed, and then everything changed.

"I was never convinced I'd get back to Nashville, but I didn't spend time on should I go or not," he told *People* Magazine. "It was just 'Not going.' Your mother had just lost a child . . . her youngest child was not going to leave the house. Chris's dying got me a little more mature."

Luke helped out as much as he could, but his parents divorced two years after Chris died. Besides playing at local bars and working for his father, Luke transferred to Georgia Southern University in Statesboro, Georgia.

College life wasn't terribly different for Luke from the life he had known in Leesburg. Sure, his new school had over 20,000 students. But the former farm college was still a lot like home. "Georgia Southern is about as rural as where I was brought up," he explained to CMT.com. "I used to laugh that I could be in class at 3:30 and be on a deer stand at 3:35."

In addition to hunting and fishing, college life offered the familiar escape of music. Luke continued to perform with his band Neyami Road. The band played two or three nights a week, and the members divided the money they earned. When the band produced their own CD, it sold several thousand copies, mainly to fans around Georgia Southern University. Even though Neyami Road was a college band playing covers, Luke was making a name for himself.

Neyami Road got a break when they opened for Ricochet. Two songs Neyami Road played that night later got recorded, "Good Directions," which became a number one song for Billy Currington, and "Tacklebox," which also became a hit and appeared on Luke's first album *I'll Stay Me*. Edward Morris of CMT.com reported, "Bryan wowed the crowd with his performance."

While at school, Luke went in a different direction from many aspiring musicians. Instead of taking courses tailored to his passion, like music theory, he majored in business. Besides attending school and playing in the band, he found time to join a fraternity. By joining Sigma Chi he was able to meet a different group of men than he met as a singer.

College life was a comfortable continuation of high school life; Luke gained more fans, but little changed. He graduated with a degree in Business Administration in 1998. Instead of going to Nashville, Luke Bryan went home.

*As an aspiring country music performer, Luke Bryan surely dreamed of nights like the one on June 4, 2014 when he joined Jason Derulo and Florida Georgia Line onstage during the 2014 CMT Music Awards.*

For Luke Bryan having a supportive partner like his wife, Caroline, made the challenges he encountered easier to deal with. Here Luke and his wife arrive at the 2010 American Country Awards in Las Vegas, Nevada on December 6, 2010.

For artists and audiences it might sometimes feel like every week brings a new awards show. Here Luke Bryan smiles for photographers in Los Angeles, California, for the 2013 American Music Awards which are awarded based on the number of votes given by fans.

# CHAPTER 3

# *Realizing the Dream*

Luke's life in his hometown was comfortable and familiar. It was also not the life he had imagined. One of his closest friends, Dallas Davidson, was an aspiring songwriter. The two often talked about making it big in country music. "We were probably just naïve enough to never think that couldn't happen," Bryan told *The Boston Globe*. As time passed it looked like Bryan's country music dreams were fading away.

Luke's mother LeClaire realized he wanted to go to Nashville, but she admitted to the ABC News Program *20/20*, "I couldn't bear the thought of him being away." It was Luke's father who told his son he could quit or be fired, but he wasn't working for the elder Bryan anymore. As Luke's father Tommy told *20/20*, "I said, 'you know, if you're going to pursue your music career, you need to pack your truck up and move to Nashville.'"

On September 1, 2001, Luke loaded up his blue GMC Yukon pick-up truck. Although he had developed a fan base across Georgia, he was not well known in Nashville. He thought he would have to start all over again. That would mean playing small bars and opening for better-known acts. It would mean showcasing (paying money to play for an audience of music executives and managers). But he got lucky.

"I didn't know a thing about it," Luke told *CMT News*. "I didn't have one contact. Then I met Rachel Proctor, who was a songwriter at Murrah Music." After playing for her, she introduced him to the owner of the company, Roger Murrah. "He really dug the songs that I was writing and decided to give me a publishing deal."

> *"None of these songs were on the radio. They were just songs he had written, and those fans were always important to the vision we had for Luke," said Cindy Mabe.*

The years of writing his own songs paid off and he had a reliable job. Even better, Luke got to meet important people in the music business.

In December 2003, Luke joined three other staff writers and played his songs in the lobby of record label BMI Nashville. When a Capital Records Nashville executive heard Luke play, Bryan was signed to a recording deal. Capital Records, which is part of the global record company Universal Music Group (UMG), did all they could to make sure Luke's first album did better than the few thousand CDs sold by Neyami Road.

The label's job became easier after UMG's executives realized Luke already had plenty of fans. "When we first signed Luke, he was playing packed college clubs around Georgia and the fans knew the words to every song," Vice President Cindy Mabe told *Billboard* Magazine. "None of these songs were on the radio. They were just songs he had written, and those fans were always important to the vision we had for Luke."

By then the executives who bought his songs had become Luke's biggest supporters. "Luke simply has that elusive 'it' factor," Mike Dungan, CEO of Universal Music Group Nashville told *Billboard*. "He is a ramped-up Elvis. His stage performance and persona are extraordinary. His genuineness and sincerity are evident in everything he does. And most important, his songs are right in the pocket. This one is going to be a force for a long time."

After half-a-dozen years in Nashville, Luke Bryan's first album was released. In February of 2007 he told The Augusta (GA) *Chronicle* that he wasn't unhappy about how

*Benefit concerts allow performers to support important causes. Here Luke Bryan performs at the "Georgia On My Mind" concert on May 12, 2015 in Nashville, Tennessee, supporting the Georgia Music Foundation.*

long it took. "If there is anything positive to gain from [Chris's death], it was God's plan. I think if I had moved to Nashville at nineteen, I probably wouldn't have been mature enough to handle everything."

For Luke, the album release made 2007 look like it would be his best year ever, but it wasn't.

> "If there is anything positive to gain from [Chris's death], it was God's plan. I think if I had moved to Nashville at nineteen, I probably wouldn't have been mature enough to handle everything," said Luke.

Luke was invited to perform at Nashville's Grand Ole Opry, a famous country music venue. His older sister Kelly Cheshire brought over one hundred people from Leesburg to watch.

Two weeks later, she was dead. Kelly was thirty-nine and had seemed healthy. "They never determined what happened," Bryan told Taste of Country.com. "The autopsies, the coroner, no one could figure it out."

Kelly's death left a husband without a wife and three children without a mother. It also left Luke feeling lost and confused. "My only older siblings . . . gone from the world in a flash in two different, crazy, tragic manners," he told *20/20*. "You can lean on friends and family . . . and you can get back [to] life."

Despite the loss, Bryan held onto his dreams. He had his first album to promote and songs he wanted the world to hear. And while many singers would have turned the deaths into sad ballads, Bryan's songs remained fun and upbeat.

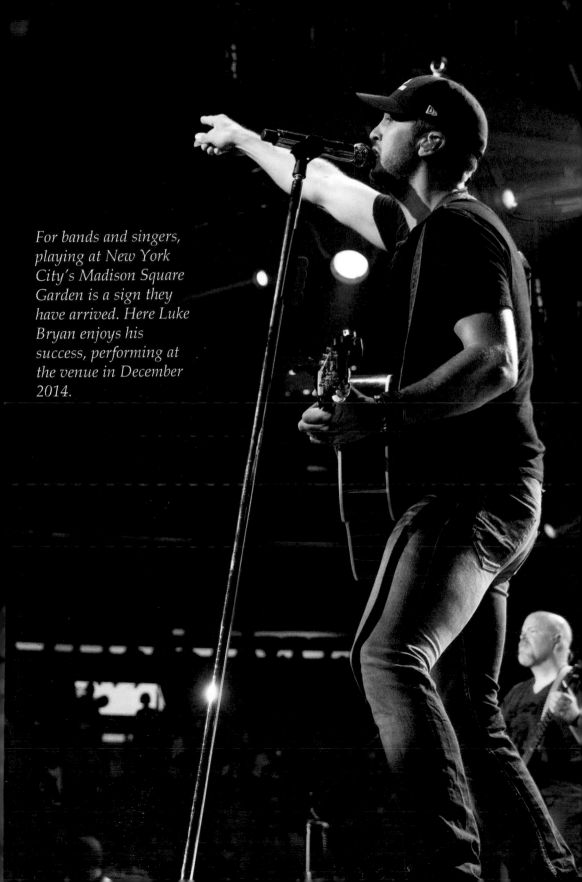

*For bands and singers, playing at New York City's Madison Square Garden is a sign they have arrived. Here Luke Bryan enjoys his success, performing at the venue in December 2014.*

Even Country Stars have to put on a jacket occasionally. Here Luke Bryan and his wife pose at the 2012 Billboard Music Awards.

# Spring Break
# Breaks Out

*L*uke's first full-length album *I'll Stay Me* attracted listeners with its catchy, upbeat songs. Reviewer Ken Tucker at *Billboard* Magazine said, "*I'll Stay Me* is the perfect title. Listening to the Georgia native sing about trucks, mama, red-eyed gravy and wrestling hogs and gators, you realize he knows of what he speaks. And that's the attraction to this fine record."

Luke's life was about more than just music. By the time his first record was released, he had a family of his own. Luke married Caroline Boyer on December 8, 2006. Two years later, their first son Thomas "Bo" Boyer was born on March 18, 2008. Bo's brother Tatum "Tate" Christopher was born on August 11, 2010.

Although *I'll Stay Me* was recorded before his sister's death, Luke's follow-up album, 2010's *Doin' My Thing* was just as positive. He developed a good sense of what songs to include on his records by how fans responded when he played live.

As Luke's album sales grew, so did his concerts. Like many performers, he began his music career as an opening act playing before the headliner—the one most fans went to see. Just as Luke's band Neyami Road drew attention from headliner Ricochet, as a solo act Luke developed his own following. He was also paired with other rising stars like Trace Adkins and Kenny Chesney.

By 2010, Bryan was ready to stand on his own. As he prepared to headline, he took a risk. Although successful bands and solo acts usually play in cities, Bryan's tour focused on rural areas. So instead of Atlanta, Luke's "Farm Tour" opened on a plantation in Statesboro, Georgia—home of Georgia Southern University. Luke's record label realized many of his fans were college students. In 2010, Luke's records connected with them in a unique way.

For decades, record labels marketed hip-hop, rock, and pop to college-age students, and country music lagged. Nashville Capitol had a solution. They would combine Luke's music with one of the biggest events in most college student's lives—Spring Break.

Every spring, students from across the country take a week after midterm exams to have fun and put the stress of school behind them. They often head south, to warmer vacation spots like Panama City, Florida, at the Spinnaker Beach Club, where Luke gave free spring break concerts. Many students played Bryan's music and loved it.

"The young college kids taught us that if we wanted to keep them, we'd have to figure a way to keep them engaged, and that was by releasing music targeted toward them, faster and more deliberate. That was the birth of the Spring Break tour and Extended Play (EP)," Universal Music Group Vice President Cindy Mabe told *Billboard* Magazine.

Beginning in 2009, Nashville Capitol released EP Spring Break Albums. With titles like *Spring Break With My Friends*, *Spring Break 3*, and *It's a Shore Thing*, they featured upbeat, fun songs—perfect for the college break.

In the Spring of 2013, the first full length Spring Break album, *Spring Break . . . Here to Party* did something no Luke Bryan record had done before—it entered the *Billboard* 200 at number one. This was not the *Billboard* Country list. The *Billboard* 200 listed the top selling albums for the week in all categories. Luke beat out pop favorite Bruno Mars, indie folk artists Mumford and Sons, and hip-hop duo Macklemore and Ryan Lewis. He even beat Jimi Hendrix, whose new album was released over three decades after his death. In a 2013 Interview with *Billboard* Magazine, Luke confessed, "It's all a dream. All I wanted to be is a big old country star and I cannot believe it's happened. It's the time of my life and I'm lovin' every day."

*Most performers prefer concert tours to recording in a studio. Luke Bryan doesn't just feed off his audience's energy — how they respond to the songs he plays helps him decide what to include in his albums. Here he performs in Bristow, Virginia, in the WMZQ Fest.*

Luke Bryan proudly displays the two trophies he won at the 2015 Academy of Country Music Awards — Entertainer of the Year and Vocal Event of the Year.

# Sadness Returns

*L*as Vegas, Nevada is better known for casinos and gambling than country music, but on a Sunday night in April it was the perfect place for Luke Bryan. When he entered the MGM Grand Garden Arena for the forty-ninth Annual Academy of Country Music (ACM) Awards, he was focused on his job as co-host with Blake Shelton.

He later admitted he barely paid attention when he was up for an award. He certainly didn't expect to beat out artists like Shelton or Jason Aldean for Entertainer of the Year. After all, he was Aldean's opening act not that long ago. Besides, Taylor Swift was also nominated. Her records had sold more copies and she was probably better known to the over one million people who voted.

Entertainer of the Year was the last award handed out that night on April 6, 2013. When Luke heard his name called, everything got blurry. In an *Associated Press* article, he admitted it was "like I was on a tilt-a-whirl." After accepting the award, he held it up, looking at it and he told the crowd, "this is unobtainable . . . You know that statue in

Pointing and smiling, Luke Bryan indicates one of the two awards he won at the 2014

Rio de Janeiro? That is what this award is like for me, up on the mount, you know."

By 2013, Bryan had already won ACM awards for top new solo vocalist and top new artist. In 2012, he won the American Country Award for male artist of the year and the American Music Award (AMA) for favorite male artist. Luke's music videos were also winning awards. He was especially proud of that, because he had directed the music videos himself.

He did not like to leave anything to chance. Maybe it was his business education, maybe it was growing up on a farm, but he rarely waited for other people to help him. Although he appeared in the music videos for songs from *I'll Stay Me*, in 2008 he directed two videos: "Country Man" and "Run Run Rudolph."

Not everyone accepted Luke's music; many felt it was too simple and too easy. Because he preferred wearing baseball caps to the cowboy hats worn by other country stars, his music was sometimes called "Baseball Cap Country." His music was sometimes called, "Bro Country" because he had been in a fraternity. Yet the negative comments did not alter his fans' support. As a CMT Senior Vice President told *Variety*, "He's as hot an artist as we have in this format."

By the end of 2014, Luke felt like he had achieved all of his dreams. He was looking forward to attending the *CMT Artists of the Year Special* on December 2. But the weekend after Thanksgiving, Luke's brother-in-law Ben Lee Cheshire passed away.

During the CMT ceremony, country stars Lady Antebellum and Chris Stapleton sang a cover of Bryan's song "Drink a Beer." The song is about remembering someone and the good times they have had together. Luke was back in Georgia watching the live broadcast and he tweeted his appreciation. "That was amazing. Truly."

# CHRONOLOGY

1976    Born Thomas Luther Bryan on July 17 in Leesburg, Georgia to Tommy and LeClaire Bryan. Luke had an older brother Chris and an older sister Kelly.

1996    Older brother Chris is killed in a car accident.

1999    Luke graduates from Georgia Southern University with a degree in Business Administration. He begins working for his father at his father's peanut mill in Leesburg, GA, and fertilizer and chemical business in Smithville, GA.

2001    Luke leaves for Nashville, Tennessee to pursue a career in country music. He begins writing songs for Murrah Music.

2004    Travis Tritt records "My Honky Tonk History," a song Luke wrote.

2005    Capitol Records signs Bryan to a record deal.

2006    Luke marries Caroline Boyer on December 8.

2007    Luke's older sister Kelly Cheshire dies at age thirty-nine. Bryan releases his first album *I'll Stay Me*.

2007    Grand Ole Opry Debut.

2008    Luke's son Thomas "Bo" Boyer Bryan is born on March 18.

2010    Luke's son Tatum "Tate" Christopher Bryan is born on August 11.

2014    Luke's brother-in-law Ben Lee Cheshire dies.

2015    Luke's tour makes some noise by selling out six consecutive stadiums.

# DISCOGRAPHY

2006    *Luke Bryan* (EP)

2007    *I'll Stay Me*

2009    *Doin' My Thing*

2009    *Spring Break With All My Friends* (EP)

2010    *Spring Break 2 . . . Hangover Edition* (EP)

2011    *Spring Break 3 . . . It's a Shore Thing* (EP)

2011    *Tailgates and Tanlines*

2012    *Spring Break 4 . . . Suntan City* (EP)

2013    *Spring Break . . . Crash My Party*

2014    *Spring Break 6 . . . Like We Ain't Ever*

2010    Academy of Country Music Award for Top New Solo Vocalist and for Top New Artist

2010    CMT Music Award for USA Weekend. Breakthrough Video of the Year (for *Do I*)

2012    CMT Music Award for Male Video of the Year (for "I Don't Want This Night to End")

2012    American Music Award (AMA) for Favorite Male Country Artist

2012    American Country Award for Artist of the Year, Male Artist of the Year, and Single of the Year ("I Don't Want This Night to End")

2012    American Country Award for Album of the Year (*Tailgates and Tanlines*)

2013    American Country Award for Artist of the Year

2013    ACM Award for Entertainer of the Year

2014    CMA Award for Entertainer of the Year

2015    CMT Award for Male Video of the Year (for *Play it Again*), ACM Award for Entertainer of the Year Shared, ACM Award for Vocal Event of the Year with Florida Georgia Line

# FURTHER READING

**Books**

Luke Bryan, *Tailgates and Tanlines* (Sheet Music). Hal Leonard Corporation, 2012.

Savage, Clarence and *Luke Bryan: 111 Success Facts-Everything You Need to Know About Luke Bryan*. Emereo Publishing, 2014.

**On the Internet**

Academy of Country Music Awards
     http://www.acmcountry.com/

Country Music Trivia, Quizzes and Fun
     http://countrymusic.about.com/od/trivia/tp/

"For the Love of Music: The Story of Nashville"
     http://www.visitmusiccity.com/storyofnashville/

Official Luke Bryan Website:
     http://www.lukebryan.com/welcome.html

# Further Reading

## Works Consulted

### Broadcast Interview

Johnston, Janice, Emily Whipp and Alexa Valiente, "Luke Bryan Opens Up about the Two Tragedies . . . " ABC News *20/20*. November 4, 2013. http://abcnews.go.com/Entertainment/luke-bryan-opens-tragedies-broke/story?id=20780322

"Luke Bryan Part Two," *YouTube Big D & Bubba*. Uploaded August 20, 2008. https://www.youtube.com/watch?v=bgj1MldBbvs

### Newspapers

"Academy of Country Music Awards 2013: Luke Bryan Pulls an Upset," *Associated Press*. April 8, 2013. http://www.cleveland.com/music/index.ssf/2013/04/academy_of_country_music_award.html

Fontaine, Janis. "'Good Directions' Writer to Entertain at the Fair," *Palm Beach Post*. January 13, 2010. http://www.palmbeachpost.com/news/entertainment/music/good-directions-writer-to-entertain-at-the-fair/nMPX7/

Rhodes, Don. "Singer-songwriter overcome's Life's Setbacks," *The Augusta Chronicle*. February 22, 2007. http://chronicle.augusta.com/stories/2007/02/22/rho_117477.shtml

Rodman, Sarah. "Luke Bryan Steps Up to Stadium-sized Success," *The Boston Globe*. August 7, 2014. http://www.bostonglobe.com/arts/music/2014/08/07/country-star-bryan-steps-stadium-sized-success/pMA02DEyrt3Vxv7QjIGkLM/story.html

## Further Reading

**Periodicals**

Atkinson, Katie. "CMT artists of the year"" *Billboard* Magazine. December 13, 2014.

Finan, Eileen. "At Home With Luke Bryan," *People*. November 6, 2013. http://www.people.com/people/archive/article/0,,20744298,00.html

Hendrickson, Matt. "Luke Bryan Takes You Home to Leesburg, Ga.: 'I Loved Growing Up Here.'" *Parade*. April 5, 2014. http://parade.com/274914/matthendrickson/luke-bryan-takes-you-home-to-leesburg-ga-i-loved-growing-up-here/

Price, Deborah Evans. "Country charmer: from sold-out 'Spring Break' tours to rocking the ACM Awards, Luke Bryan is country's next poster boy." *Billboard* Magazine. March 28, 2013.

**On the Internet**

Anderson, Danielle. "Watch Luke Bryan's 'Roller Coaster' Video." *People* Magazine. June 20, 2014. http://www.people.com/article/luke-bryan-roller-coaster-video-premiere

Luke Bryan Biography—All Music.com http://www.allmusic.com/artist/luke-bryan-mn0000502198

Maness, Jessi, "Luke Bryan and the Team Behind the Fame." *Sports & Entertainment Nashville*. May 7, 2014. http://sportsandentertainmentnashville.com/luke-bryan-and-the-team-behind-the-fame

Morris, Edward. "Luke Bryan Takes the Long Road to Fame," *CMT News*. January 8, 2008. http://www.cmt.com/news/1579286/luke-bryan-takes-long-road-to-fame/

Ventura, Amanda. "Out of 23 of his official music videos, two are self-directed: 'Country Man' and 'Run Run Rudolph,' both in 2008." *AZ Sports & Lifestyle*. http://azsal.com/celebrities/doin-my-thing/

Vinson, Christina. "Luke Bryan Raises a Beer to his Late Siblings with 'Drink a Beer' at 2013 CMAs" *Taste of Country.com*. November 6, 2013. http://tasteofcountry.com/luke-bryan-siblings-drink-a-beer-cma-awards/

Whitaker, Sterling. "Luke Bryan's Brother-in-Law Passes Away." *Taste of Country*. December 1, 2014. http://tasteofcountry.com/luke-bryan-brother-in-law-dies/

# INDEX